T0129225

Life Jackets

Weathering the Storm

Glenn A. Gelabert

WESTBOW
PRESS®
A DIVISION OF THOMAS NELSON
& ZONDERVAN

Scripture quotes are taken from the King James Version of the Bible.

WestBow Press books may be ordered through booksellers or by contacting:

WestBow Press
A Division of Thomas Nelson & Zondervan
1663 Liberty Drive
Bloomington, IN 47403
www.westbowpress.com
1 (866) 928-1240

ISBN: 978-1-5127-9046-7 (sc)
ISBN: 978-1-5127-9045-0 (e)

Library of Congress Control Number: 2017908845

Print information available on the last page.

WestBow Press rev. date: 06/14/2017

Smart Strategies is
proud to introduce

*Life Jackets: Weathering
the Storm*
by Glenn A. Gelabert

"Fear not"
will be found
365 times in
the Bible.
What was
God trying
to tell us?

For I know the plans I have for you. Plans to prosper you not harm you. Plans to give you a hope and a future. — Jeremiah 29:11

If you're not passionate about what you do, do something else.

Your tongue is the rudder of your ship. Where are you headed? Guard your tongue.
—James 3:4

Have a personal pep rally each day.

Speak to your problems with positive affirmations.

Do not let
the sun set
on your
anger.
—Ephesians
4:26

The best study—
hope.
The best day—
today.
The best
thought—peace.
The best way to
get to heaven—
faith.

Know this too shall pass.

Be receptive. Keep an open mind.

Get uncomfortable. You should be comfortable being uncomfortable. This will cause you to grow!

Life is not about circumstance. It's about how you deal with circumstance.

Lead by example.

All things are possible through Christ who strengthens me.
—Philippians 4:13

Everyone deserves a second chance.

Nothing is sadder than a wasted talent.

Your talents and your blessings are gifts from God. What you do with them is your gift back to God.

Be a light in the midst of darkness.
—John 1:5

Two roads diverged in a wood and I—I took the one less traveled by, and that has made all the difference.

—Robert Frost

A dead end is just another place to turn around.
—Judith Albright

F.E.A.R.

**False
Evidence
Appeared
Real**

Fear Not.

Be resilient. Bounce back.

Work to obtain balance in everything you do.

Geese fly 72 percent farther by staying in formation. Stay in formation!

Take responsibility for your actions. Give up "would've," "could've," and "if only."

Your words should edify or build up. The rule is build up or shut up.

Goals must be S.M.A.R.T.

Specific

Measurable

Attainable

Reasonable

Trackable

Do unto others, as you would have them do to you.
—Luke 6:31

Don't wear too much cologne. Remember, your cologne should not get there before you do.

Laughter adds years to your life.

Take it to the source. Don't gossip.

60 percent of what you say does not come out of your mouth. Be aware of your body language.

Don't get in
the mud.

Learn an attitude of gratitude. If you have a flat tire, be grateful you have a car.

Enthusiasm— the God in you.

It does not matter how many times you fall down; it only matters how many times you get up.

If you have been sucking on a lemon most of your life, stop it!

It takes many muscles to frown, and only one to smile. Start smiling more often.

If you have twenty dollars in your bank account, you have more wealth than 85 percent of the world's population.

It takes ninety-nine praises to offset one criticism.

In order to get respect, you must first give it.

Believing is seeing.

Faith is the substance of things hoped for, the evidence of things not seen.
—Hebrews 11:1

Be happy with what you've got, but never be satisfied.

Always have a purpose. A man at the age of sixty-five who retires without a purpose will die in the first year.

Make a good first impression. You can only do it once.

If you want to be an eagle, you must fly with eagles. If you want to be a pigeon, go to the plaza.

In order to find a friend, you must first become a friend.

Reconcile with loved ones when they are living—it's harder when they are dead.

If you have a
friend who
says life is
miserable and
we are just
waiting to go
to hell, get a
new friend!

If you really want to get at someone who has harmed you, forgive them!

Eat vegetables.

Take good care of your body. You only get one.

Practice kaizen—constant, never-ending improvement.

Be kind and loving to your children; they did not get to choose their parents.

Know that you are worthy.

Be kind to the elderly—you will soon be one!

A wise man once said the best way to deal with procrastination is to put it off.

Savor the victories of life. Celebrate small successes.

Life is a long-distance run, not a sprint.

When you pray, pray as if you have already received it. That alone is a step of faith.

When you
know why
you do what
you do, you
do it better.

**Do all things in moderation.
—Ephesians 5:18**

Perform one act of kindness each day.

Call your mother and tell her you love her.

Become a better listener.

Give and it will be given unto you.
—Luke 6:38

Get organized. Organization reduces stress.

Raise your expectations, for you get what you expect.

**Giving.
When you give,
God will bless
you back—and
you can't out-
give God!**

Pray for your enemies. —Matthew 5:44

If God had a wallet, your picture would be in it.

Dance like no one is watching. Love like you have never been hurt.
—William W. Purkey

Stop complaining!

Celebrate life. You only get one.

Printed in the United States
By Bookmasters